C000001811

DON'TS
FOR GOLFERS

Uniform with this Volume

—

DON'TS FOR WIVES
DON'TS FOR HUSBANDS
DON'TS FOR GOLFERS

—

A. & C. BLACK, LTD

DON'TS
FOR GOLFERS

BY

SANDY GREEN

LONDON
A. & C. BLACK, LTD.
1925

Published September, 1925.

INTRODUCTION

ONCE upon a time there was a worthy Minister o' the Kirk who started to learn golf late in middle life. He soon discovered that the art of smiting the elusive guttie is not quite as simple as it appears ; and he was further surprised at the ease with which expressions of feeling quite incompatible with his cloth issued from his lips. On his return to the Club House one of the members hailed the Minister: "Well, Minister, I *heard* you in your last bunker. What do you think of the game?" The Minister shook his head sadly, and blushed to think of what the other had overheard. "I'm afraid I'll hae to gie it up," he replied.

"What? Give up golf?" asked the member. "Na, na!" replied the Minister, striding once more towards the first tee ; "I'll hae to gie up the Meenistry!"

Now, this is an example of the proper spirit in which the game should be tackled, though, with the help of these few "Don'ts," it may not, perhaps, be necessary for the reader to go to the same extreme as our Scots divine. These "Don'ts" are compiled from practical experience and from the "wise saws and modern instances" of the Masters of the Royal and Ancient Game.

SANDY GREEN.

DON'TS FOR GOLFERS

DRIVING.

DON'T move your head while making a shot.

Don't grip your club tightly with *all* your fingers. The thumbs and forefingers are the important "grippers."

Don't disturb your balance when swinging back from the ball. Let the club-head lead, the arms following.

Don't lunge forward with your arms as you start the downward stroke. Let them swing round in their own way from the apex of the swing.

Don't be afraid of hitting hard. If your swing is all right, you will not press, however hard you hit.

Don't begin by practising the most difficult shots. Master the easy shots first, and, whether you are a mere beginner or a "just-so-so" player, your game will improve. Most scratch players agree with Vardon that the easiest shots are those from the tee with a brassie, or from the fairway with an iron.

Don't think that by using the brassie from the tee you are neglecting the use of the driver. The driver and the brassie are used for making a shot from the tee, or from a good lie on the course, in precisely the same manner. Only, as the face of the brassie has a

slightly greater loft, it will give the
beginner a feeling of confidence if he
uses it at first from the tee.   The
practice gained thereby will stand him
in good stead when later on he is
called upon to make use of the brassie
from the fairway.

Don't make the mistake of having
a high tee. The less sand you use in
making the tee the better.   The ball
should be seen apparently just clear of
the ground perched upon nothing.

IRON PLAY.

Don't forget that the iron and cleek are shorter in the shaft than the brassie and driver. It is well to remember that the shorter the shaft, the nearer to the ball should be your stance.

Don't indulge in undue bending. Draw a little closer to the ball.

Don't stoop more for cleek and iron shots than for drives. For the cleek shot the feet are nearer together, and for the iron a little nearer still.

Don't forget to aim behind, not directly at, the ball when making a cleek or iron shot. Select a spot a fraction of an inch behind the ball ;

the space between the ball and the grounded club is the spot on which your eye should be fixed at the completion of the address.

Don't neglect the important rule of keeping the head still, just as in swinging with driver or brassie. This is an all-important rule to be remembered in connection with every club. That is why it is so often mentioned.

Don't begin to use the cleek until you are thoroughly at home with the iron. As the brassie is to the driver, so is the iron to the cleek.

Don't grip your club so savagely that you get into a state of inflexible tautness, or you will become muscle-bound. A slightly firmer grip is desirable for the iron clubs, as they have a tendency to turn in the hands at the moment of impact with the ground. But if you remember the forefinger and thumb the other fingers will automatically follow with the amount of increased pressure desirable.

Don't hug your arms to your sides because you are standing a little nearer to the ball. Let your arms be clear. Govern the length of your shot by the back swing.

Don't, when a half shot is required, take the club right back and then try to prevent the ball going too far by checking the club at the moment of impact. Always hit the ball unhesitatingly.

Don't lift the body when hitting. This often follows a tendency towards crouching when addressing the ball in iron and cleek shots.

MASHIE SHOTS.

Don't make the mistake of treating the mashie as an easy club on account of its loft. It is a club that requires most delicate handling. Daily practice with a mashie will prove to you what a friend or fiend the mashie can be, according to the amount of respect you pay to the observance of its proper treatment.

Don't forget that the success of a mashie shot depends chiefly upon the movement of the knees. The "pivoting" is all done with the knees in the mashie shot. The feet must not move from the ground, except that the right foot may be turned on to its inner side at the moment of impact, but without moving that foot from position.

Don't try to scoop your mashie shots. Hit quite freely ; the club will provide the loft.

Don't be in a hurry to look up. There is a natural tendency when approaching to see immediately how near to the objective the ball has travelled. Keep the head still until the follow through has well started.

Don't forget the value of "cutting" with the mashie when you are afraid that the ball will run too far.

Don't, in cutting, be afraid of trying to draw the face of the mashie sharply across the ball at the moment of contact. And remember that the place to aim for is a yard or so to the left of the pin, as a ball, if properly cut, will screw to the right on touching the ground.

Don't discount the value of a pull when you want to play a low shot that will rise slightly on the rough ground and finish on the smooth with a run. This can easily be done by striking the ball cleanly at the back, and, at the moment of impact, slightly turning over the right hand.

Don't overdo the turn of the right hand in the pull, as the fraction of an inch too much is apt to have a devastating effect.

BUNKERED.

Don't be downhearted. If you keep your nerve, the bunker is often much less formidable than the rough.

Don't attempt too much. Be content with taking the easiest way out. There are occasions, of course, when desperate cases require desperate remedies ; but, as a general rule, "safety first" is the game to play for the bunkered.

Don't be afraid of trying for distance in getting out, if your ball is teed up or, at all events, lying on a flat, clear space in the bunker. Make due allowances for the nearness of the face of the bunker, and hit out cleanly with the club most suitable for the occasion.

Don't try to hit the ball out of the ensconced position. Take the sand or other substance about an inch and a half or two inches behind the ball with your club, and don't bother about a follow through. The stroke should end with the niblick-head buried in the bunker. The less distance you want to go the more sand you take.

Don't fail to hit hard.

Don't forget that you cannot go too far into the sand with your niblick.

Don't imagine that your niblick will cut straight down into long rough grass

and at the same time raise the ball.
It won't. Aim well behind the ball;
the grass will be cut by a following
through shot.

PUTTING.

Don't be nervous. Putting is largely a matter of confidence.

Don't let the hole overpower you. A dread of not being able to putt out when only a few inches from the hole is largely responsible for dozens of those missed putts.

Don't worry as to how you should use your putter. There is no fixed rule. Find out which particular method of sending the ball into the hole comes easiest to you, and stick to it.

Don't be careless. Remember, once again, that your head must be kept still.

Don't move your body. The fingers and wrists are alone sufficient to give the proper pendulum movement to the club.

Don't disregard the old maxim, "Never up, never in." Hit the ball firmly. Don't look up till you have finished your follow through.

Don't examine the line to the hole from both ends. It only confuses you. You see so many possible lines that you will end by choosing the wrong one.

Don't lose sight of the fact that a partner who can putt calmly and accurately is a valuable asset when playing in a foursome. You have only nine drives apiece, but there are eighteen greens where both you are your partner are likely to be called upon to wield the putter.

Don't be content to lay the ball dead when putting. Play for the hole. There's always a chance of the ball going down, and you might as well lie on one side of the hole as the other if the putt doesn't come off.

Don't let your attention wander when your opponent is putting first. You will get valuable information as to the pace and slope of the green from watching the course of your opponent's ball.

Don't underrate the effect of the wind on your ball, especially if it is a bumpy green. On a fast green the wind influences the ball to a much greater extent than on a slow one, but with a bumpy green the wind catches the ball as it leaves the ground at each little jump.

Don't forget that when there are two slopes to be reckoned with on the green, it is the slope nearer the hole that affects the ball most. The reason for this is that the ball will be travelling more slowly when it reaches the further slope.

Don't raise your putter further from the turf than you can help on the back swing. Follow the shot through in the same way, and always remember that the face of the club must be absolutely square to the hole.

Don't vary your putter. Get to know it and make it like part of yourself. If you find that you have, after repeated experience, gone to pieces with your putter, practise for a bit with a heavier one. You will not be able to swing it so quickly, and a slow, steady pendulum-like swing is half the battle in putting. Then get back to your original putter and hope that you have overcome your failing.

Don't run away with the idea that putting with any other club except the putter is against the rules. There are occasions—certain stymies and putting down a sloping green—when a mashie or iron can be of much greater service to you than the regular putter. The great thing is to get the ball into the hole.

Don't step either on the line of your opponent's or your own putt. The hole can be claimed by your opponent if you do.

FAULTS.

Don't be unduly depressed about topping. It is a trouble that can be fairly easily eradicated by paying attention to the actions that cause it—*i.e.*, moving the head, pulling the arms up at the moment of impact.

Don't spare any endeavour to eradicate the unintentional slice. It is a fault whereby you lose distance. A sliced ball will not travel far. Check any tendency to lean towards the right during the upward swing. Make up your mind that the clubhead must always commence the

movement both in the upward and
downward swings.

Don't be lured into believing that
pulling is a harmless fault. It is, in
strict moderation, as a pulled ball certainly travels. But remember that
the least over-pull may land you in a
nasty lie and cost you a valuable
stroke. Pulling is often caused by
uneven gripping.

Don't try to cure a pull by develop-
ing a slice, or vice versa. If you do,
you will only end by being hopelessly
involved as to where you are really
aiming.

Don't change your mind at the top
of your swing as to how you are going

to carry out your shot. A "foozle" will result. Make up your mind when you address the ball as to what you mean to do with it. Keep your head still and do it.

Don't overdo the excellent old adage "Slow back." It is sufficient to bear in mind that the club should not travel faster on the upward swing than you can stop it at any given point. "Slow back," if overdone, is upsetting to the balance. There is a happy medium.

Don't forget that with all iron clubs, when the ball is about to be taken the club must meet the ground squarely.

Don't stand too near or too far from the ball. The proper distance is that from which the sole of the club, from toe to heel, is completely resting on the turf when the club is grounded.

CLUBS.

Don't be afraid of being thought "swanky" because you have a decent set of clubs and a sensible bag with a hood on it. Even if you are not a scratch man there is no reason why you should not be properly equipped.

Don't, if you are a novice, rely on your own judgment when buying a set of clubs. Be guided by some experienced player or a good professional. If you cannot find such a one to guide you, buy clubs stamped with the name of a good professional.

Don't be niggardly as regards the price of a club. Pay a good but fair price ; it will be more economical in the long run.

Don't rush off to buy every new patent club that is put on the market. Mistrust the club guaranteed to "do anything."

Don't waste money on patent grips. Provided the grip is comfortable and the balance right, the thinner grip you have the better.

Don't buy a club that is too heavy. Choose one that feels just heavy enough to have some force behind it.

Don't buy iron clubs that are dissimilar as regards "lie," the putter, of course, excepted.

Don't neglect the shafts of your clubs. Many players expend much labour on keeping their iron clubs

dazzlingly polished, and entirely over-
look the fact that a little oil on the
shafts will do much to preserve their
clubs.

Don't forget that a small quantity
of some good furniture polish rubbed
on the shafts of your clubs in wet
weather makes an excellent preserva-
tive dressing.

Don't risk a driver or a brassie shot
in wet weather without first giving the
face of your club a rub with a piece of
chalk. This will absorb the moisture
and prevent skidding when you strike
the ball.

Don't take only your favourite clubs
with you when you go out for a practice. Take those you like least. They

are the ones you most need practice with. It is, however, a good plan to take one of the trusty favourites with you just to vary the monotony and make you feel that, when things are at their blackest, you are not an absolute dud with every club.

Don't use coarse emery paper for cleaning your clubs. If you are uncertain of your caddie, let him clean your clubs only with natural sand or the very finest of fine emery paper.

Don't turn up your nose at the man who has a bag full of unpolished clubs. More than one first-class player refuses to play with bright clubs. There is probably quite a lot in the theory that the roughened surface gives more control in contact with the ball, and there is also the glitter of the polished steel to distract the eye from where it should be focussed.

Don't set out without a few first-aid implements for your clubs in the pocket of your golf-bag. A tack or two, some binding thread, and a roll of rubber sticking plaster are very useful in case temporary repairs become necessary.

Don't rattle your clubs in the golf-bag more than you can possibly help. If you do, the varnish on the shafts of the longer clubs will be destroyed by coming in contact with the heads of the shorter ones.

Don't throw your golf-bag down violently. Your clubs are not to blame for your bad play. They have done you no injury ; why should you injure them ?

IN THE CLUB HOUSE.

Don't forget the Club House is a social institution. Make the newcomer welcome, and see that he does not feel out of it when you old cronies are fore-gathering before the "day's work" has begun. The same applies to the time when tales of doughty deeds on the links are being exchanged at close of play.

Don't let there be any snobbishness in the Club. If a man is good enough for election as a member, he has every right to *enjoy* the privileges of the Club.

Don't bore the other members by recounting in detail every phase of your game. It doesn't interest them in the least to know why you foozled your drive on the fourteenth tee, or how the worm-cast diverted your putt when you only wanted one for the match.

Don't clump into the dressing-room on a damp day without first having scraped the superfluous mud off your shoes. You would show more consideration for your own domestic staff. Why show less for the servants of the Club?

Don't monopolize a lavatory basin for longer than you absolutely need. There are others who want to have a wash and brush-up before lunch. Give them a chance, and wait until you get home to have a thorough bath.

Don't corner all the periodicals and papers in the lounge. You cannot possibly read more than one at a time, and the other fellow will be glad to swop with you after you have both finished.

Don't encourage grousers by listening to and sympathizing with all their trivial grievances. Turn them on to the members of the Committee. They will know how to deal with the man who has a chronic grievance. If it is a legitimate complaint, the Committee will deal with it in the natural course of the Club's business.

Don't monopolize the entire fireplace on a cold day. There is plenty of room for everyone if you like to make it. In any case, it is bad for you, and productive of chaps and chilblains, to crouch over the fire.

Don't turn the Golf Club into a Bridge Club. A quiet rubber is all right when the weather is too bad for a round of golf, but don't waste precious hours when you might be out on the course.

Don't try to persuade the Steward of the Club to do anything contrary to the Law of the Realm or to Club Rules. If he is a good chap he is anxious to do all in his power to please you, but it is unfair to expect him to risk his job because you have a "between hours" thirst.

Don't indulge in recriminations towards your late partner in a foursome. No doubt, if your joint efforts to win have met with dismal failure, there is much you both feel like saying. But get it all off your chest before you come into the Club House.

Don't neglect to look at the Notice Board. It is no use grousing when told about some new rule for local play, because you knew nothing about it, if you don't take the trouble to read all the official announcements.

Don't be for ever trying to get up a gamble on your own or anybody else's game. An occasional sweepstake is amusing, but the man who is always offering to bet on this, that, or the other is a terrible bore.

Don't carry on conversation at the top of your voice. Somebody may want to hear you, but the fellow who is reading or thinking out his tactics for the forthcoming competition certainly does not. At the same time—

Don't whisper. Short of the bellower, nothing is more irritating than the person who whispers confidentially to his vis-à-vis in a corner.

CLOTHES.

Don't wear boots if you can accustom yourself to the use of shoes. Shoes give freer play to the ankles than boots ; and as your swing depends to a certain extent on the turn of your left ankle, it is as well to wear nothing that will impede the movement of the ankle muscles.

Don't wear shoes or boots that are not perfectly comfortable when you put them on before starting the game. If they are not comfortable before you set out, you may be sure that they will be more uncomfortable before you have reached the eighteenth hole.

Don't wear footgear that makes you feel conscious of your feet. Remember that your one thought must be to place the ball to your best advantage, and that is an impossibility if you are pre-occupied in any way.

Don't neglect to keep your golf-shoes in good condition. Use some good dubbin or oil to keep the leather waterproof and pliant.

Don't put wet shoes away in your locker without having first put them on lasts or trees. If you have no trees handy, stuff the toes with paper—anything to keep hard ridges from appearing across the instep.

Don't wear crêpe shoes on a wet day. You will slip on the short grass if you do.

Don't hold crêpe soles too near a fire. Should the corrugated surface of the rubber become worn, it is a good plan to score the sole with a hot wire or poker.

Don't have tackets put in clumps upon the soles of your shoes. You will get a better grip of the ground if there is a space of about three-quarters of an inch between each tacket.

Don't wear shoes or boots that are too thick in the sole. There should be a certain amount of give, so that you can, when necessary, rise on your toes.

Don't constrict your neck with a tight collar. You will find that, when the collar is too tight, your head will

move to one side when you are taking
your back swing. Once again, "Remember to keep your head still."

Don't wear a collar that is too high.
Something about one inch in height is
near enough the mark.

Don't sport a necktie that flaps
about. If you are wearing a long tie,
see that it is fastened down securely.
Nothing is more distracting than a tie
that suddenly whips into your face
just as you are at the top of your
swing.

Don't wear new braces. Keep a
special pair of braces in your locker,
and never mind how old they look so
long as your nether garments are kept

up and your shoulders allowed sufficient free play.

Don't constrict your waist with a tight belt. If your waist muscles are tightly bound up and your shoulders free, you will probably over-swing. Vardon advises braces in preference to belts.

Don't wear more clothing than your actual comfort and convention demand.

Don't irritate your opponent by wearing jazzy colours. To dazzle his eyes with a multi-coloured pull-over or peace-disturbing golf stockings is to take a mean advantage.

Don't play in gloves if you can avoid it. If you must play in gloves, wear a pair made of soft wash-leather and allowing plenty of room. Palmless mittens, however, keep the hands as warm as gloves, and are much better for your grip. Have a pair with three loops—one for the first finger, one for the little finger, and one for the thumb.

Don't stuff your pockets with too many odds and ends. But if you carry a rubber-cored ball in your pocket, the heat of your body will "buck-up" the resiliency of the rubber core. It is quite a useful tip to play two balls alternately, keeping the one warm in your pocket while the other is in play.

Don't wear a hat or cap that impedes your line of vision or distracts your eye from the ball.

Don't worry about the plus-fours or trousers controversy. Wear whichever you feel are most comfortable. Plus-fours are certainly to be recommended as far as freedom for the knees and ankles is concerned.

LADIES.—Don't try to play golf in an afternoon confection. This is uncomfortable, besides being bad form.

Don't wear thin silk stockings with sports-clothes. They are bad for the feet, and they look wrong.

Don't wear high-heeled shoes. They ruin your balance as well as the putting-green.

Don't wear jewellery likely to impede your swing or restrict your grip.

In any case, pearl necklaces and diamond rings and pendants do not improve the appearance of your sports suit.

GENERAL MAXIMS.

Don't lose heart because you have made a bad start from the tee and your opponent has got away with a clean, straight drive. A hole is never lost until it is won.

Don't lose an opportunity of playing a round with a good player. You'll learn much more from losing holes to a superior player than from winning them from someone inferior to yourself.

Don't play golf until you have learned the rules of the game. If you know them and play up to them, you will be justified in expecting your opponent to do the same.

Don't be the first to give up the search should your opponent lose his ball.

Don't play with a dirty ball. A sponge in a rubber case is not a costly acquisition, and will probably save you many aggravating minutes of search, not to mention lost balls. But—

Don't forget to see that the sponge is moist before starting out.

Don't play with old balls. Even though it is still quite white and very nearly new, a rubber-cored ball is often a dead 'un.

Don't take any risks if you are playing in a very close match. It may sound unsporting, but it's the way to play the game.

Don't underrate the value of winning the first hole. It is as valuable as the eighteenth.

Don't fail to mark down the exact spot where your ball has found the rough. If you are careful to make a habit of this, you will save time and money.

Don't neglect to replace a piece of turf that someone else has cut up and omitted to replace. Your ball may find that spot some other round.

Don't hold others back whilst you are searching for a ball. Let them through, and

Don't start pressing them if you should recover your ball the second after you have allowed them to pass.

Don't fidget while your opponent is teeing up and addressing his ball. The least movement is disconcerting And

Don't make a sound. You can easily wait to clear your throat after your opponent has finished his stroke.

Don't let your caddie annoy your opponent by doing anything that you would not do yourself.

Don't praise your game to your caddie. He has no doubt got his own opinion, and it is more comfortable for you to leave it at that.

Don't ask for a "half" if you are ever so near the hole. Let the suggestion come from your opponent.

The short putt is one of the most
nerve-wracking experiences in golf.

Don't forget your partner when
playing in a foursome.   Consult him
should he be a superior player to yourself.   If he is the weaker player, don't
expect too much from him.   Remember
you are playing for pleasure, and avoid
making him feel he is letting you
down.

Don't declare, after you have been
beaten, that you have played a dis-
gustingly bad game.   Let your opponent have the satisfaction of his
victory.

Don't disparage your own play if
you are the winner.   Let your opponent

think that it has been quite a tough struggle.

Don't sympathize with your opponent if he makes a bad shot, but

Don't forget to notice his good ones.

Don't insist on having a ball or money on a friendly match. Some people will gamble on anything, but if you can't enjoy the game for its own sake, you'll never be a golfer.

Don't keep up a running fire of conversation during the round. Golf is a game in which thought is necessary and silence is preferable to chatter.

Don't play too much golf. Two rounds are quite sufficient for one day at any time.

Don't let yourself get stale. If you find your game is going badly to pieces, forget Golf altogether for a little while, and you will find yourself better able to tackle the problem when you start again. Too much worrying as to whys and wherefores results in hopeless foozling.

Don't be over-anxious when negotiating a difficult shot. If you take things easy, the chances are all in your favour, but if you worry, you are sure to do something wrong. On the other hand,

Don't imagine that thought is not required for every stroke. It is. And if you can think a few strokes ahead, so much the better. Try to plan out your attack for each hole.

Make up your mind before each stroke exactly where you want your ball to land and play for it.

Don't make your opponent feel that you are watching him in case he infringes any of the rules. And don't appear to be counting his every stroke. You will have quite enough to do in looking after your own score.

Don't wait until you reach the hole before you start reckoning your strokes. Count each stroke as it is made. You will be much less likely to make an error in counting if you do.

Don't argue with your opponent as to his scoring. Take his word for it and accept defeat gracefully.

Don't tear up your card in despair unless you are positively certain that you are hopelessly beaten. Golf is a game in which "a buddy can never be shair."

Don't "give" anything when you are playing for a team. If when playing on your own you care to be generous, that is entirely your own affair. But when playing for a team you are not playing for yourself, and the team expects you to WIN.

Don't spoil your caddie for other people by over-paying him. If he manages to retrieve your ball from a water hazard or puts himself out in some other way, you are, of course, justified in giving him a small tip. But ordinarily, by tipping you are making it difficult for some less affluent player on future occasions.

Don't grouse about stymies. They are part of the game. Most stymies are not insurmountable difficulties. You can with practice manage to get round or over your opponent's ball provided always that you don't imagine a stymie is an impossible position.

Don't be shy about taking out a scoring-card. Even if you are not playing a serious game, it is useful to get into the habit of recording your strokes, and it gives you some sort of standard to strive for.

Don't ask the advice of your caddie and then deliberately disregard it. If he is your regular caddie, he knows

your game better than you do yourself, and in any case, he has probably
had more recent experience of the
condition of the links than you have
had.

Don't, if you have followed your
caddie's advice, reproach him should
the shot fail to come off. It will make
him chary of advising you again, and
he will only feel that the fault lies
rather with your bad execution than
with his theory.

Don't, on taking the pin out of the
hole, dig it into the green.

Don't throw down your golf-bag on
the green so that it is likely to come
into your or your opponent's line of
vision while in the act of putting.

Don't use the wrong kind of confidence. The right confidence is that which makes you feel that with practice you will one day be able to play golf. The wrong kind of confidence is that which makes you feel you would really be a first-class golfer if you could only be bothered to practise.

Don't practise yourself stale. Practise until you feel more or less confident of being able to repeat a given shot at a given time, and then enjoy a good game.

Don't worry when you have been given a hint as to the playing of a particular shot, or some instruction as regards your swing, because your game is temporarily interfered with.

Until you can adopt the method sub-consciously, the apparently destructive effect is almost bound to occur. Persevere until you can do the thing without thinking about it.

Don't think of the difficulties that beset you on either side of the fairway and of the bunkers that yawn between the tee and the green. Make up your mind that so long as you keep your head still and your eye on the ball, there is nothing to hinder your hitting a straight shot that will not be penalized.

Don't experiment when you are playing a match. Keep all experimenting for the practice games. In match or medal play make the most of the shots in which you have the greatest confidence.

Don't let ambition interfere with judgment. Once you have mastered all the golf shots the resulting game is determined by the amount of judgment you use in the application of the shots. Find out your limitations and don't give way to the temptation during a match to chance your luck in bringing off, just for once, some stroke that you have never done under normal conditions. You can minimize your limitations by practice.

Don't lose your temper, neither with your opponent, nor the caddie, nor the golf-clubs, nor, above all, with yourself. If you are playing a rotten game, don't take it too seriously. After all, it is a game, and you will only make it an unpleasant one if you let yourself become unpleasantly serious over it.

Don't despise a hint from your caddie because he is merely "a wee bit laddie." Most of those youngsters have acquired more first-hand knowledge of the game from caddying for good players than you will ever assimilate from a textbook.

Don't forget that an ounce of practice is worth a pound of theory. Read all the golfing books you can, but getting hold of everything the greatest exponents of the game have ever written will not do you a ha'porth of good unless you practise.

Don't despise style. May beginners are content with swiping the ball along in any old way, but style is merely the crystallization of all that makes for accuracy and control.

Don't blame your clubs for faults of your own that may be easily corrected if you analyze your methods of using the implements. If, after careful testing, a club continues to disappoint you, try using a different one. It is no use struggling on with a club in which you have no confidence.

Don't lose your head because you have missed the ball completely. On the contrary, keep your head steady when you repeat the stroke. Many novices are so flustered when they foozle that they it wildly and widely not once but several times.

Don't be downhearted because you have sustained a bad beating. There are "off days" in which nothing seems to go right. Try to remember the spots where your luck has apparently been right out. You will probably find that it was not so much that luck failed you as that you failed to play the shot properly. Cheer up and correct the fault the next time out.

Don't make Golf your sole topic of conversation. There are a few otherwise quite intelligent persons who are non-golfers. You will never make converts if you bore non-players to

distraction by for ever talking of the
Royal and Ancient Game.

Don't miss the beauties of Nature by
becoming too absorbed in this game.
It will add greatly to your pleasure
and improve your play if occasionally
you rest your eyes on the landscape.

Don't tire the tyro. The average
player who plays regularly is in good
training and can do the two rounds a
day with perfect ease. But when
taking out a beginner bear in mind
that the raw recruit uses up three or
four times the amount of physical
energy through not playing properly,
and blistered hands and aching legs
and arms will be the result of trying
to do too much.

Don't have a caddie unless he is a good one. A good caddie is always worthy of his hire. A bad one is a constant irritation. Carry your own golf-bag rather than risk adding another stroke a hole to your game by employing a poor caddie.

Don't forget the etiquette of the game any more than the rules. You may make yourself exceedingly unpopular by adhering strictly to the rules if you neglect the courtesies of the game.

Don't buy golf-balls from a caddie or any other person unauthorized to sell them. It is a good plan to have some distinguishing mark stamped on your ball, and to make a point of returning all balls found on the course to the caddie-master. Somebody may do as much for you.

Don't be afraid of offering a game to another member who is without a companion. Many lasting friendships have begun with a round of Golf. If your handicap is a long one, you may learn some useful tips to shorten it, and if you happen to be the better player, you will improve the other man's game.

Don't hurry unduly if you are playing from a crowded first tee ground. Waste no time in taking your place, but don't let the fact that others are watching you make you forget "slow back and keep your head still."

Don't race away after your ball the minute you have finished your follow through.   Mark carefully the spot where it has landed and then walk at your normal pace in that direction.

Don't bother about the exact spot on the teeing ground where you mean to place your ball.   Seek rather to find a good place for your feet.   The tee will make things all right for your ball, but there is nothing to help your stance except the feel of the ground to your feet.

Don't practise swinging near the teeing ground when other people are addressing their balls.   The sound of your club is disturbing to the ear, even if you are well out of the line of vision.

Don't drive out of your turn. Be particular when the honour is your opponent's that he should have it, and be equally particular in playing first should the honour be yours. It is an often forgotten fact that the man who plays first is pioneering, and that to play second is to receive valuable information regarding the wind, the speed of the fairway, and the distance required.

Don't let your game break down when victory is almost within your grasp, because your opponent, though unable to get on the green in two, holes out for four. Remember, it is the steady player, who is never flurried and fights in the face of adversity, who will carry all before him.

Don't indulge in a hefty lunch and afterwards expect to be in top form for an afternoon round. Eat a moderate meal and rest yourself in an armchair for at least half an hour before setting out again. You'll easily save that half-hour on your game if you are not too stodged.

Don't gulp down a long cold drink in one draught if you are thirsty during a hot day's golf. An excellent way of assuaging your thirst is to rinse the mouth with cold water without swallowing more than you can help. If you feel you must swallow it, take it in small sips.

Don't forget that the rules of Golf entitle you to remove certain obstacles.

Remember this when you are playing: even if the obstacle does not actually interfere with your stroke it is liable to catch your eye and distract your attention.

Don't open a blister on your hand by pricking it in the centre. Sterilize a needle by holding its point for a few seconds in the flame of a match and then run the point under the uninjured skin into the blister. You can draw off the water by this means without actually breaking the blister, and the skin will not peel off before the under-skin has lost its tenderness.

Don't hold the wrong thought. To think at the beginning of a game that the result will be against you is to encourage that result.

Don't over-indulge yourself in eating and drinking during the non-golfing days, and then expect to work off excess by "a good game of Golf." You may play Golf of sorts, but it will not be a good game. Physical fitness is as important for Golfing as for any other sport where co-operation of mind and muscle is required.

Don't strain your eyes. If you are in the habit of wearing glasses, use wide lenses, preferably rimless. The rims are rather inclined to take your attention from the ball while you are swinging the club.

Don't let your muscles grow stiff and set if you are unable to get a fair amount of practice with your clubs. A few simple physical exercises every morning will keep you supple, and if you have space to swing a club indoors, do so. It is a good plan when indoor-swinging to use a piece of crumpled paper in place of a ball, as it is better to have something to swipe at.

Don't be too tense between the shots. You will be better able to concentrate when the right moment comes if you let your mind relax and take things easy until then.

Don't be temperamental. Golf is a game of nerve as well as skill. In match play the moderately good golfer

who can command his nerve has a
tremendous advantage over the bril-
liant player who becomes "jumpy"
when playing before an audience. As
Andrew Kirkaldy has it, the right
temperament for winning matches is
"just commonsense."

Originally published 1925
Republished 2008 by A & C Black Publishers Limited
38 Soho Square, London W1D 3HB
www.acblack.com

ISBN 9781408106716

A CIP catalogue record for this book is available
from the British Library.

Printed by WKT Company Ltd, China